THE CHRISTIAN'S GUIDE SERIES

The Christian's Guide series is the result of a strong conviction that there is a need for a series of short, simply-written books, dealing with basic Christianity —its doctrine and its practice—designed for the ordinary Christian.

If the Christian Church is to be faithful to her task of evangelism in this generation, every Christian needs to be a missionary. To accomplish this worthy objective, the Christian must understand the gospel and be able to explain its relevance, as well as believing its message.

This series is written with the situation and needs of the busy church member in mind. Such a purpose accounts for the conciseness of the books. The authors —who are chosen deliberately from different denominations—aim to be Biblical, practical and contemporary in their writing. The first purpose is to discover what God has to say on each subject. Then, where the subject is a practical one, to put the emphasis on the *how* rather than on the *ought*. The faithful application of the principles of the Christian life, laid down in the Bible, to life today is a foremost aim.

DEREK PRIME

BOOKS IN THE CHRISTIAN'S GUIDE SERIES

Edited by The Rev. Derek Prime

*Other subjects in active
preparation*

JOHN B. TAYLOR

A CHRISTIAN'S GUIDE
TO
THE OLD TESTAMENT

HODDER AND STOUGHTON

PRINTED IN GREAT BRITAIN FOR HODDER
AND STOUGHTON LIMITED, ST PAUL'S HOUSE,
WARWICK LANE, LONDON, E.C.4 BY C. TINLING
AND CO. LIMITED, LIVERPOOL, LONDON AND
PRESCOT

Contents

1 WHY AND HOW

    Many Christians neglect the Old Testament. They find it difficult to read and even more difficult to understand. In comparison, the New Testament is easy: the Gospel stories of Jesus Christ never grow stale, and the Epistles are full of helpful teaching about the Christian faith and how to live it out.

The Old Testament, however, seems to present many problems when it is first read. Genesis for a start brings one face to face with the age-old conflict of science versus the Bible. Other books too have their difficulties, not least because we know so little about the background and customs of the people who are being described. What are we to make of Solomon's private life, for instance, with his many wives and concubines? Or else we fail to understand the meaning of certain prophecies because we don't know enough about the historical situation in which they were uttered. And some books, like Job and Ezekiel and Nahum, to name just three, are so hard to make sense of in the Authorised Version that we soon give up and move elsewhere. Only the Psalms and parts of

Isaiah are easily appreciated. So, with the limited time available for Bible reading, the New Testament gets read and the Old gets left.

Now we don't often own up to thoughts like these because we feel somehow we shouldn't think them, but they lurk beneath the surface. The purpose of this little Guide is to help to make the Old Testament easier to read by filling in a few of the more obvious gaps in our knowledge. We shall begin by listing four good reasons *why* the Christian ought to read the Old Testament, and then we can get on to the subject of *how* he should do it.

□ Why read the Old Testament?

Answer number one: Because it was the Bible of Jesus Christ and the Apostles

Our Lord knew the Old Testament Scriptures so well, reading and memorising them so that they became a part of Him. Through them He learned the Father's will for His ministry and His eventual death. The whole pattern of His life and behaviour was undergirded by the deep conviction that "the Scriptures must be fulfilled" (Mark 14: 49). For Jesus, what the Bible said, God said; it was God's voice, clear, inescapable and true.

Those who would discredit the Old Testament argue that Jesus merely absorbed the outlook of the Jews of His time regarding the sacred writings, and that He was the child of His age. If so, He was a very critical child, for the religious experts of the day met no more searching critic than the Prophet of Nazareth. He denounced their narrowness towards those who were not Jews, He denounced their hypocrisy, He denounced the finicky way they interpreted the Scriptures, but He could only endorse the esteem in which they held their Old Testament. It was undeniably the Word of God.

Answer Number Two: Because it Gives Meaning to the New Testament

The Gospels and Epistles abound in allusions to the Old Testament and in technical terms and metaphors which can only be understood against an Old Testament background. Take for instance the matchless description given by John the Baptist of Jesus: "Behold the Lamb of God, which taketh away the sin of the world" (John 1: 29). For us the lamb is a symbol of meekness and childhood innocence, but John the Baptist had before him the Old Testament picture of a helpless animal being offered as a sacrificial victim at the Temple in Jerusalem to atone for human sins, and this clearly was the significance he was attaching to Christ.

An appreciation of this point makes all the difference to our understanding of that central fact of our faith, the death of Christ. If we think of the Cross simply as an illustration of innocent suffering, that is to say, regarding Christ as the Lamb of God in the modern sense, then our view of His death is little more than a sentimental admiration for a remarkable act of submission. But if we understand the Lamb of God in its true Old Testament sense, we see in the Cross the sacrifice offered for our sins, we see Him dying in our place and we worship Him as our Saviour and Sin-bearer.

Answer Number Three: Because it gives Christianity a Historical Setting

The centre of Christianity is an event in history; it happened under Pontius Pilate that Christ was crucified, dead and buried. But God had been active in human history long before His coming, and the Old Testament tells of all that led up to the birth of the Messiah, God's chosen Saviour.

In this story there are three focal points: the call and choice of Abraham to be the forefather of God's people, the divine deliverance of the exodus and the crossing of the Red Sea under Moses, and the restoration of the exiled Jews from the Babylonian captivity in the sixth century B.C. All these were historical incidents which stand out like mountain peaks on the canvas of the Jewish background to the rise of Christianity.

Unlike other religions which are mainly built around the views of one great man, the religion of the Bible looks back to actual historical events when God did something tremendous. The Old Testament tells the story of the great things God did before Christ was born, and the New Testament tells of His greatest act in sending His Son to live and die for mankind.

Christianity is not just a set of ideas, a code of living or an explanation of the meaning of the universe. It is much more than that. It is God intervening in His world to save it.

Answer Number Four: Because with the New Testament it Makes up the Bible

The Bible is God's unique revelation of His purpose for mankind. The Old Testament contains not only a description of God's acts in history: it contains also the explanation of His acts in prophecy. The deeds and the words go hand in hand. So too in the New Testament, the event of a provincial prophet's crucifixion under irregular circumstances and after a trial of doubtful legality *means* nothing, without the accompanying explanation which it was given by Our Lord Himself and by His apostles after Him. Gospels and Epistles tell the facts and explain their meaning.

The Old and New Testaments are bound up together in that both explain things the same way. They tell of the same God, the same way of salvation (in the Old foreshadowed, in the New achieved), the same demand for repentance and faith as the only way to God's favour and blessing. They are thus inseparably linked together, as the old jingle has it—

The New is in the Old concealed,
The Old is in the New revealed.

□ *How to read the Old Testament*

Most of us in our younger days made the great decision to read the Bible all through. We begin at Genesis chapter 1 with high hopes of reaching the end of the Book of Revelation in some three years' time, at the rate of a chapter a day, but few of us weathered the storms of Leviticus, and the idea died on us as quickly as a New Year resolution.

For the young Christian, Old Testament reading needs to be selective, and one of the merits of a daily Bible reading scheme lies just here. But we should not be satisfied simply with devotional reading of ten or fifteen verses a day. The Old Testament needs to be read in longer sections than, say, the four Gospels. A shorter book, like Jonah or Amos, needs to be read at one sitting if possible, in order to get a general view of its contents before the slower meditative study of it section by section. A longer book like Genesis or Jeremiah may have to take five or six sittings, but it is most important that the overall picture is seen first. A survey of the wood is a valuable preliminary to an examination of the trees.

This swift reading is best done in the Revised Standard Version of the Bible, an American translation published in 1952. (For details of other translations of the Bible, see *A Christian's Guide to Bible Study*, pp. 57 ff.). Where the Authorised Version's seventeenth-century language is often difficult, the R.S.V. is readable and in many cases represents a more accurate translation. You can buy an inexpensive paperback copy now, and it has the advantage of a good-sized print which is a pleasure to read.

It is also useful to precede this preliminary reading of a book with a glance at the introductory summary of its contents and message that you will find in a one-volume Bible commentary or a small Bible dictionary. But this is not essential.

What is essential is some background knowledge of what the Old Testament is all about. What is it trying to say? What help can it give to twentieth-century Christians who are pushed for time? How can I get the most out of my Old Testament?

The following pages are intended to help right here. In the next chapter we are going to look at a Hebrew family to see how they lived eight hundred years before Christ, to get something of the atmosphere of the Old Testament. Then we shall take a bird's eye view of the panorama of Old Testament history, so that we can see the whole picture in perspective. Chapter four will be a detailed look at the books of the Old Testament one by one to introduce us to what they contain and what they teach. And finally we shall include some pages on the general message of the book and how it fits in with the message of the New Testament.

Last of all comes a suggested course of reading to help you to get down to the job straightaway. It is really the most important part of the whole book.

2 ISRAEL AT HOME

Tucked away in the back-streets of the city of Ramah, five miles north of Jerusalem, you will find the tiny one-roomed dwelling where Benaiah lives with his family. He lives much the same sort of life as the people round about him, never far from starvation level, cooped up in the city through the cold rainy months of winter and longing for the springtime when he can get out into the fields and work his ground.

He is a gentle, God-fearing man and he is proud of the way his wife Rebekah has been training his children in the same paths. So many of the people in Ramah have abandoned the worship of the Lord and have taken up with strange new gods like Anu and Ishtar of the Assyrians. One or two had even erected altars to them on the roof of their houses. Benaiah was afraid because he knew that sins like that would not go unpunished, and they might one day wake up and find an enemy at the gates of their city.

Ramah was a small city with a population of only about six hundred, including children. In times of danger or in the bad weather they were all herded together within the walls in an area of only a few acres. Benaiah's family had to share their one room with two goats and a sheep. Even though there was a raised platform for the family's living and sleeping quarters, they were glad when the weather permitted them to climb up on the roof and get some clean-smelling air. On the rooftops the children could run about and play and Rebekah could talk with the neighbours. It was a good place for gossip too and you only had to mention something on the rooftops and it was round the city like a flash (see Matthew 10: 27). Not that there was much opportunity for gossiping because Rebekah was an industrious wife and spent most of her day working down below.

The day began early. The animals saw to that. Sarah, the eldest daughter, went off down the narrow alleys, dignified by the name of streets, to draw water from the city's spring. When she got back with a full water-pot balanced on her head, she found that her sister Hannah and their mother had already ground some barley and were waiting for her return to mix it with water and leaven to make the day's batch of bread. Benjamin, the youngest, had been unwillingly coerced into lighting the fire under the oven—really a woman's job, he thought! The oven was nothing more than a large, saucer-shaped bowl that was upturned over the fireplace.

When the oven was hot the flat barley-cakes were placed on top to bake, rather like crumpets on a hot-plate. They had to be turned and done on both sides or they were very indigestible. The prophet Hosea said that the people of Ephraim were "like a cake not turned" (7: 8), so he must have known!

Meanwhile Benaiah and Eli, the eldest son, had gone out through the city-gates which opened at sunrise and were making their way with scores of others to their small plots of ground. Benaiah's strip, his "portion", had been in the family for generations. Originally it had been quite a sizeable field, but as each generation died it was divided up between the sons and now he was hard put to it to keep his family on its produce. Certainly, when he was gone, Eli and Benjamin would not be able to manage on it. Unless something could be done they would get swallowed up by the larger landowners as so many of his fellow-citizens had been. It was not a bright prospect.

Today they did not stay in the fields all day because Benaiah had some business to do in "the gate". This was the open space just outside the city-gates where everything went on. Here wares were bought and sold, the blind and the crippled begged, the unemployed waited for someone to hire them, the greybeards sat and talked, and those who had been wronged came to ask for justice from the city elders.

Benaiah wanted to buy some corn because his own supplies were running short. He always dealt with a man named Reuben, because he knew he could be trusted. Reuben's measure was a full-sized ephah and didn't have a false bottom like those used by some of the corn-merchants. He gave good measure too, "pressed down, shaken together and running over"

(Luke 6: 38). When the right amount had been measured out Reuben took out his balances and his weights which he put in one pan while Benaiah weighed out his silver into the other. It was common practice for the less scrupulous traders to falsify their balances with extra heavy weights, but Reuben was never deceitful upon the weights so Benaiah had no fears (see Deuteronomy 25: 13-15; Proverbs 20: 10, 23; Micah 6: 11). The transaction over, Benaiah scooped up the grain in a piece of cloth and prepared to move away.

Just then the elders of the city walked out through the gates to hold court and to hear complaints. No sooner had they appeared than a young woman recently widowed ran forward pleading for justice and telling a long and involved story about some money she owed to a merchant and how he was threatening to sell her small children into slavery if she didn't repay it by the next new moon. When the merchant's name was mentioned there was a gasp from the crowd who had gathered round, because he was one of the wealthiest and most feared men in the city. Would the judges do justice or would the rich man's money win the day? It was a long case: witnesses were heard and questions asked, but eventually the judges reached their verdict. The woman was vindicated and her family's safety was ensured, at least for the time being.

Benaiah was glad as he walked back home. This was pleasing to the Lord when the fatherless and widowed were protected. Maybe the righteousness of the judges would make up for the deceits of some of the merchants and the rooftop shrines of some of the people. Maybe Ramah would be spared after all.

As the evening drew on Benaiah was tempted to return to the gate to join the men of the city in conversation. There was nothing more pleasant than to sit there and discuss the events of the day. The old men who spent the best part of every day there knew everything that was going on, the strangers that had arrived, the disputes that had been settled, and the news of the world outside. It was good to hear them talk and to learn from their experience. Sometimes they would swap anecdotes or pass on clever proverbs or riddles they had heard, and Benaiah would try to memorise them so that one day when he was older he would have some wise words to speak in the gate.

But tonight he stayed at home because tomorrow called for an early start to the day. It was a festival and he wanted to go up to Jerusalem for it. The sun went down and everything slept.

For beds the family shared two straw mats which were laid on the bare, earthen floor; for blankets they used the cloaks which were their normal outdoor garb. The little oil lamp burned dimly on a ledge in the corner. It was never allowed to go out except when the fire was alight in the daytime. It was the only box of matches they had! However, it gave very little light and so once you had settled down for the night it was impossible to get up without waking the whole household (farmyard and all!) and a late night caller was never welcome. Compare the parable Jesus told in Luke 11: 5-8.

The next day Benaiah took Eli to Jerusalem, Benjamin being considered still too young to go. As they walked towards the holy city they found themselves unconsciously lapsing into songs like

> "I was glad when they said unto me,
> Let us go into the house of the Lord."
>
> (Psalm 122: 1)

The roads were thronged with worshippers, because even though this was not one of the three major festivals—Passover, Weeks and Tabernacles—there were always plenty of loyal believers who would make the journey, especially from the cities round about Jerusalem. Benaiah loved to see the crowds at festival time. It renewed his confidence in God to share in these great acts of worship, and even young Eli felt twice the man.

They joined in the psalm-singing, they watched all the sacrifices being offered—their own offering was a mere brace of pigeons which Benaiah bought on his way into the temple, but then they didn't have the money that some people had. One of the priests took the birds, wrung their necks and let the blood trickle down by the side of the great altar of sacrifice. Then with a deft movement with a knife he disembowelled the carcases, threw away the crop and tail feathers into the ashpit, and then walked up the steps to throw the remains on to the fire. There was a brief sizzling, a puff of smoke and it was gone.

"Our gifts seem very small to God," Benaiah

assured Eli, "but He wants them just the same. It's the only way we can show that we care for Him."

"Why do they have to die?" asked the boy.

"Why, to remind us that we deserve to because of our sins, but God says that He'll accept these instead." They stayed a while to pray and watch, and then walked away.

In the outer court of the Temple a crowd had gathered near one of the gateways. Benaiah hurried over, wondering if he was going to have the rare pleasure of hearing Isaiah or Micah uttering one of their prophecies. It was Isaiah, a gaunt, upright figure whose eyes glowed with passion as he prepared to speak.

"Woe to those who join house to house,
who add field to field,
until there is no more room
and you are made to dwell alone in the midst of the
    land. . .
Woe to those who are heroes—at drinking wine,
and valiant men in mixing strong drink,
who acquit the guilty for a bribe,
and deprive the innocent of his right!"

(Isaiah 5: 8, 22, 23)

Eli listened enthralled. He had never heard anything like this before. Benaiah was nodding his head. "There are not many like him," he said, "who speak up for the working man. But he'll land himself in trouble if he goes on like that."

20

They moved round the crowd to where some scribes were sitting down writing. Benaiah could not write and he was always intrigued by those who could. They were using writing-tablets that were hinged in the middle and on the inside waxed surface they were writing in columns from right to left with a reed pen tipped with metal. They explained that they were disciples of Isaiah and they spent most of their time following him around, taking down his prophecies and repeating them to others who had not heard them. Benaiah suggested that they ought to visit Ramah some time.

"We have some good people in Ramah, but there are quite a few who need to hear what Isaiah has got to say," he added.

And he said it again several times over to Eli as they made their way home later that afternoon.

In case you think that this imaginary episode is an insult to your intelligence, let me say that one of the most important things to learn when you read the Old Testament is that it was written for the benefit of ordinary peasant folk who lived like Benaiah and his family, who could neither read nor write but who could listen, and who had a simple but profound trust in the Lord God of Israel. They were God's people.

So away with all your twentieth-century world of newspapers, supermarkets and space travel. Try to think yourself back into the past and listen to the message of the Old Testament as if you were Benaiah himself—or Rebekah, as the case may be.

3 GOD AT WORK

If you go into a library you will expect to find books grouped together according to their subject-matter: travel in this corner, science over there, religion usually tucked away on two or three low shelves that you have to squat down to look at, and all the novels and fiction books in serried ranks round the walls.

The Old Testament is like a library. It consists of thirty-nine books and they have been grouped together according to their subject-matter: history, prophecy, poetry and so on. They are not necessarily in the correct historical order, but as we shall see later they are arranged in a careful logical pattern. Now before we try to sort them out it will be very helpful to get a broad outline of the history covered by the Old Testament and then we can put the books into their rightful places on the way. That is what we are going to do in this chapter.

The fascinating thing about the Old Testament is that its history is not merely a matter of dates and doings in the past. It is a living story telling of God at work in the life of a nation, the people of Israel. So when we read it we look out first and foremost for what it contains about God and His plans for His people. If we read it in any other way, we shall miss the point.

☐ The Family of Abraham

Abraham was the father of the Jewish race, and every Jew thinks and speaks of himself as 'a son of Abraham'. Actually, Abraham had two sons, Ishmael, whose mother was the slave-girl, Hagar, and Isaac who was born to Abraham's lawful wife Sarah. Although it was normal procedure in those days for a childless wife to give her husband a hand-maid so that children could be born into the family, the Bible makes it clear that Abraham was wrong to do this and Ishmael was therefore the result of a union which was displeasing to God. The reason is simple. God had promised to Abraham that He would bless him in a special way and give him a son by Sarah despite her advanced years, and that through this "child of promise" there would eventually be a vast family of descendants to enjoy the promised land of Canaan and to be God's chosen people (Genesis 17: 8).

So today the Jew traces his ancestry back to Abraham via Isaac, and considers himself to be the heir of the promises made to his far-distant forefather. Whether he is right or wrong to think like that is a matter we will look into later. The important thing for now is to remember that the history of Israel is the story of how God's promises to Abraham worked out over the centuries from Abraham to Christ.

There were three parts to the promises:

1. A promised son—Isaac, through whom would come a nation "as the stars of the heaven and as the sand which is on the seashore".
2. A promised land—Canaan, corresponding roughly to all modern Israel and parts of Jordan as well.
3. A promised relationship—they were to be God's chosen people, and He was to be their God.
(See Genesis 12: 1–3; 13: 14–17; 15: 1–6; 17: 1–8; 22: 15–18; and you will understand how vital these promises were in God's plan for Abraham)

The promised son duly came, but Abraham's faith was severely tested both before and after Isaac's birth. For a start, Sarah was sceptical about the whole story and treated it as a bit of a joke (Genesis 18: 12); then she was nearly lost to a neighbouring chieftain named Abimelech, thanks to Abraham's faint-heartedness (Genesis 20). Later on, when Isaac was growing up, the final test of Abraham's faith came when God challenged him to prove his devotion by sacrificing Isaac on a hilltop in Moriah. At the last minute God intervened and provided a ram to be sacrificed in his place. So not only was Sarah kept alive to bear her son and Isaac kept alive to marry and raise children, but the promises of God were kept alive as well.

The promised land did not fully come to Abraham.

He and his family lived in tents like Bedouin tribesmen of today and wandered from place to place finding pasture for their sheep and cattle. With his flocks he had the run of Canaan but he never possessed it in the way God intended, and when he died, the only plot of ground he actually owned was a field near Hebron which he had bought from a local Hittite landowner so that he could bury Sarah's body there in a cave. So important was this purchase—the first piece of the promised land to be owned by God's people— that the Bible gives a whole chapter to describing it (Genesis 23).

The promises were not only to Abraham but to his descendants after him. They were transmitted from father to son, but not necessarily to the eldest son. Isaac for instance had the twins, Esau and Jacob, and before ever they were born the Lord told Rebekah their mother that "the elder would serve the younger", that Jacob was the one chosen to be the heir of the promise. From the story in Genesis it looks as if Isaac never took this word from God seriously, for if he had given Jacob his God-given rights there would have been no need for the deception and scheming on the part of Jacob and his mother to secure for him the birthright and the blessing which were due to him. You can read these famous stories in Genesis chapters 25 and 27.

Jacob had twelve sons, Reuben the eldest and Benjamin the youngest. These were the founders of the twelve tribes of Israel. But again Reuben was passed over, Judah was the inheritor of the promises (Genesis

49: 9–12) and Joseph, his father's favourite, was God's chosen one to save his family from the famine and settle them in Egypt until the time should come for the promised land to be possessed under Joshua.

How does this remarkable story fit into history? We cannot say definitely, but archaeology has helped us to see that the conditions and customs reflected in the Book of Genesis fit the events into the first half of the second millennium before Christ, i.e. 2000–1500 B.C. If you think of Abraham as flourishing about 1850 B.C., you will not be far wrong.

□ *Egypt and the Promised Land*

The description of Joseph's captivity in Egypt and his phenomenal rise to power in the land reads almost as if it is too good to be true, but when you realise that from 1700 to 1570 B.C. Egypt was ruled by the Hyksos kings, who were not Egyptians but Semites, you can see that the appointment of a fellow-Semite like Joseph is not at all incredible. The way his life-story is told in Genesis 37 to 47 shows quite remarkably how Joseph's career was over-ruled by God, and the patient faith which he exhibited even in the most difficult of situations is one of the finest Old Testament illustrations of the verse in 1 Peter 5: 6: "Let yourselves be humbled under the mighty hand of God, that in due time He may exalt you."

Joseph and his brothers all died in Egypt, but their descendants prospered under the favourable rule of the Hyksos kings until eventually they came to an end. Then "there arose up a new king over Egypt who knew not Joseph" (Exodus 1 : 8). As a result of his oppression of the Israelites God raised up Moses to lead the people out of Egypt into the promised land.

It was a long time from the great days of Joseph to the great days of Moses, maybe as much as four hundred years. They are 'hidden years' as far as our knowledge of the history is concerned. But they were sufficient for the family of Jacob to emerge as the nation of the children of Israel.

Moses had been brought up in the royal palace but he also spent a considerable time as a shepherd in the Sinai peninsula (Exodus 3 : 1). There he not only received his commission from God at the burning bush, but he also came to know the desert intimately—where there was water, where a large company could camp safely and so on. It was this knowledge which came in so useful when his great moment of leadership came. Moses avoided the direct route to Canaan along the shores of the Mediterranean for three reasons. First, it was the obvious route and he could have been overtaken too easily had Pharaoh changed his mind, which of course he did. Secondly, the route passed through territory of the Philistines, who were a notoriously warlike people (Exodus 13 : 17). Thirdly, it would involve running the gauntlet of the advance Egyptian troops on the frontier at the little "river of Egypt" (the modern Wadi el-Arish, two-thirds of the way to Gaza).

The route taken therefore was south-easterly, and

the shallow waters near the Bitter Lakes, north of the Gulf of Suez, were crossed successfully thanks to the miraculous coincidence of a strong east wind, which parted the waters enabling the Hebrews to cross quickly before the pursuing Egyptians. Common caution would have warned the Egyptians, with their horsemen and chariots, to make a detour northwards to catch up the runaway slaves further along the route, but they plunged recklessly into the returning tide and were destroyed, leaving the children of Israel to make their escape free from fears of any further pursuit.

Side by side with the momentous events of the exodus comes the description of the giving of the Law to Moses at Mount Sinai or Horeb. The heart of this was the Ten Commandments engraved on two tablets of stone, but in addition there was a large collection of regulations for the life of the new nation as they prepared for their entry into the promised land. God was giving His people a fresh start.

In later years they felt that in a sense they were being born again as a nation through these dramatic experiences. They were being saved from a life of slavery and led into a new life of liberty and blessing. As you read the story of the interminable complaints and grumblings, the disobedience and downright idolatry of the children of Israel, which accompanied these acts of salvation, you will proberly pause and think of the mocking and scourging, the cruelty and treachery, which accompanied that greatest act of salvation which God performed through His Son

Jesus Christ, to whom the whole Old Testament story is a pointer.

After the years of wandering in the wilderness, the children of Israel entered Canaan, also by a miraculous crossing—this time of the river Jordan, and Joshua set about a carefully conceived plan of campaign against the inhabitants of the land. From the narrative in the Book of Joshua and with the help of a Bible atlas we can see the way he struck at strategic centres of enemy resistance. First he tackled Jericho, dominating the Jordan Valley and the key to the mountain region to the west. Then he performed a flanking movement to the north to attack Ai and struck southwards at the heart of the hill country. Some cities were left, like Gibeon and Jerusalem, but the fortresses that guarded the approaches to the land, like Makkedah, Lachish and Hebron, were picked off and overpowered one by one.

The conquest was not completed by Joshua but it was sufficient for him to disperse the twelve tribes in their appointed areas where they were each given the responsibility of consolidating their own positions.

□ *The Judges, Samuel and Saul*
      After the death of Joshua, the Israelites went through a low period. Their twelve tribes became disunited, and were ill-equipped for the uphill struggle of subduing their territories. From time to time, God raised up from one of the tribes a leader who showed particular gifts of generalship, and led his

people successfully against the enemy nations who were constantly harrying them. These leaders were described as Judges, but their function was not so much legal, as military and religious. A better word for them would be 'liberators'. They included men like Gideon of the tribe of Manasseh, who drove out the Midianites, Jephthah of Gilead who fought the Ammonites, Samson of Dan whose exploits against the Philistines make heroic, though not always edifying, reading, and the prophetess Deborah who united the three northern tribes under Barak against the Canaanites.

But apart from the exploits of the Judges, things were in a poor state in the new-won land of Canaan. Idolatry was on the increase, and the debasing influences of Canaanite religion were infecting Israelite life. Archaeology bears witness to a general destruction of Canaanite settlements towards the close of the thirteenth century B.C. followed by a period of a degenerate culture, and this is clear confirmation of the picture as given in the books of Joshua and Judges.

Two hundred years after the capture of Jericho, the leading figure in the life of Israel was not a judge but a prophet named Samuel. His leadership was distinctly religious rather than political, and he was accepted as such throughout the whole of Israel. "All Israel from Dan even to Beer-sheba knew that Samuel was established to be a prophet of the Lord" (I Samuel 3: 20).

At this time the common foe was the Philistines who inhabited the coastal plain between Gaza and modern Tel-Aviv. In the most significant military operation of the time the Philistines defeated Israel at Aphek (c. 105 B.C.), captured the Ark of the Lord and penetrated as far as Shiloh, the religious centre of the day. Never was there felt a more pressing need for a strong military leader in Israel and on the insistence of the tribes Samuel anointed Saul to be king over the united people.

For all Saul's ability, no one can say that his reign was an outstanding success. He was a man of commanding appearance and a dashing warrior, but his self-will soon brought him into head-on collision with Samuel, and Samuel was told by God to anoint David, the youngest son of Jesse of Bethlehem, as king in succession to Saul. This did not mean that David was immediately a contender for the throne, only that his ultimate succession was assured. But Saul became insanely jealous of him and showed signs of serious mental disorder. Through all this time and while David was in hiding and temporary exile, he remained remarkably loyal to Saul as God's anointed king, and continued to fight the Philistines and the Amalekites with a privately-raised army of friends and malcontents.

King Saul was an unusual character, in many ways very much like his New Testament namesake from Tarsus, better known as the apostle Paul. Both men belonged to the tribe of Benjamin, both had tremendous natural qualities. Though one was tall and handsome and the other was short and unprepossessing, both were gifted with great drive, energy and leadership. But there the comparison ends, for Saul of Tarsus was converted on the road to Damascus and learned submission to the will of God. Saul never did. He knew that God had instructed Samuel to anoint him as Israel's first king. He was God's anointed, and he was unquestionably 'on the Lord's side'. But either because he realised that he was only a kind of second-best (Samuel made no secret of his belief that Israel didn't need a king if only they had greater faith in *God's* leadership), or else because his greatness turned his head, Saul never learned to submit to God and to put His will first. His unhappy, disordered life is a constant warning to all who get thrust into the limelight without a full surrender of their lives and power to God. (See Romans 12:3.)

☐ *David and Solomon*

When Saul and his sons were killed at Gilboa (c. 1005 B.C.) resisting a determined Philistine attack, David returned to Hebron where he was received as king. He set about the task of establishing a united kingdom, which involved him in a good deal of bloodshed with rival captains contending for power, but at last he was successful. His first great achievement was to capture the hitherto impregnable fortress of Jebus, which he renamed Jerusalem, the City of Peace, and this won him immense prestige and a new capital city into the bargain. The Ark of the Lord, which had been the symbol of God's presence with His people since the days of the wilderness wanderings, was brought up to Jerusalem amid great rejoicing and David made it clear that he was going to lead his people in the worship of Jehovah according to the ancient covenant of Moses.

David is one of the great characters of the Bible: talented, popular, creative and deeply devoted to the Lord. His head was not turned in the way Saul's had been, and the reason is surely to be found in his own devotional life, the mainspring of his whole being. In many of the psalms we catch a glimpse of his close walk with God and it is undoubtedly this which kept him true. When he did sin, as in his lust for Bathsheba, which led him to do away with her husband Uriah the Hittite, the Bible does not attempt to make excuses for him but recounts the story in full detail, as if to remind its readers that godliness does not make a man immune to temptation. In the best of men are the seeds of the worst of sins. If you read Psalm 51, David's prayer of penitence, you will see that he learned his lesson and found forgiveness in the end.

Just as important as David's concern for God was God's concern for David. The third promise made to Abraham, you will remember, was of a *promised relationship* with his descendants. God had kept this promise all through the low water of Israel's history— in Egypt, in the wilderness and under the Judges— and had preserved His people, often in quite miraculous ways. With David this promise was made more definite still.

"Your offspring. . . shall build a house for my name, and I will establish the throne of his kingdom for ever. I will be his father, and he shall be my son. . . And your house and your kingdom shall be made sure for ever before me; your throne shall be established for ever" (2 Samuel 7: 12–16).

From now onwards the promised relationship between God and His people was centred in David's royal line, which would never die out and would one day produce *the* Anointed King, the Messiah, who would save His people from their sins.

Under David's inspired leadership the armies of Israel were outstandingly victorious. In every direction frontiers were extended and neighbouring nations were brought to heel. Israel was at the pinnacle of her strength and prestige. But David was less successful in ordering the affairs of his own household, where his failure to establish a clear order of succession resulted in intrigue, murder and heartbreak when his son Absalom was put to death by the over-zealous commander-in-chief, Joab. Only on his deathbed did David finally confirm his decision to make Solomon king in his place (965 B.C.)

On the human level Solomon's greatness lay in his powers of administration. He organised the extensive kingdom which his father had built up, he built a navy and promoted trade with other nations and made wise political liaisons, he instituted vast building projects throughout the land. His crowning achievement was his building of the Temple in Jerusalem, possibly on the very spot where centuries before Abraham had offered up his son Isaac. This magnificent building was to be the centre of Israel's religious life and was the God-given symbol to future generations of

Jehovah's presence among His people. As long as the Temple stood, God was in their midst.

The latter part of Solomon's reign was marked by religious decline. The king indulged his love of luxury with a vast harem and he pandered to the wishes of his foreign wives and concubines by allowing all kinds of religious practices which eventually exerted an insidious influence upon his own heart. "It came to pass, when Solomon was old, that his wives turned away his heart after other gods: and his heart was not perfect with the Lord his God" (1 Kings 11: 4).

□ *The Two Kingdoms*

After his death in 925 B.C. the northern part of the kingdom, which had always resented the fact that David and his successors were southerners from Judah, and who were particularly incensed at the unfavourable treatment they had been receiving from Solomon, broke away under Jeroboam, and formed themselves into a separate state. Rehoboam, Solomon's heir, was all for fighting to bring them back into his kingdom but he was restrained by a word from God to a prophet named Shemaiah. From that time onwards the greatness of Israel was finished. In its place were the two minor kingdoms of Israel in the north and Judah in the south.

Jerusalem was in the southern kingdom, so to offset its influence Jeroboam enlarged the northern religious centres of Dan and Bethel, introducing golden calves into the sanctuaries there. The purity of northern religion was thus doomed, and the religious focus was from then on centred on Judah. The Books of the Kings tell the story of the succession of rulers of both kingdoms, but the northern capital, Samaria, was overrun in 722 by the Assyrian armies under Sargon II and only Judah remained. Israel had been a useful buffer against the Assyrian invaders for many a year, but now the land was depopulated and colonised by non-Semitic people from other parts of the Assyrian empire. This mixed population came to be called the Samaritans and in later years played a significant role in the religious life of Palestine.

Israel's religious policy was not, however, without its opponents. When King Ahab was doing his worst to establish the Baal-cult from Tyre, God called Elijah, and after him Elisha, to stand up for the truth against these idolatries, and their influence was great. So much so that their nominee, Jehu, became king after Ahab's death and put an end to Baal-worship in the land. But he went no further, and when at last Samaria fell, it was seen as a fitting punishment for two hundred years of consistent disobedience to God.

Judah's fortunes rallied once she was left alone as the sole witness to God's truth. Under kings like Hezekiah and Josiah, reforms were instituted to clean up the nation's religious life. Of these, Josiah's was the most thorough and most remarkable, for in the year 621 B.C., in the course of a great restoration programme on the fabric of the Temple, a copy of the long-forgotten book of the law was discovered by the High Priest, Hilkiah. This was part, if not the whole, of the Pentateuch, the five books of Moses, and its discovery profoundly influenced Josiah's later reformation.

Judah's days, however, were numbered and the growing power of Babylon was soon to reach out in her direction. Not that Babylon was interested in such a third-rate power, but Judah was on the route to the real enemy in the south, the Egyptians. As long as the people of Judah were submissive to Nebuchadnezzar and paid their tribute, all was well. But twice they tried to throw off the yoke and with dire consequences. The first time in 597, King Jehoiachin was taken into captivity to Babylon, along with all the nobility of the land, among them the young prophet Ezekiel; the second time, in 586, the city of Jerusalem was rased to the ground, Temple, palace, walls and all, and all the people who survived the long siege were deported into captivity. Thus began the tragic years in Exile. But what was in one sense a disaster was in another sense a formative time for the Jewish people.

□ *The Exile*
To the people of Judah the exile was as much as anything a spiritual crisis. Disobedient though they often were, they had the idea deeply ingrained within them that they were Jehovah's people, that He was their God, and that He dwelt among them in His holy Temple. For centuries the prophets had been chiding them, pleading with them and threatening them about their way of life, but it

had never registered deeply. As far back as the eighth century B.C., when Israel was still in existence, prophets like Amos and Hosea, Micah and Isaiah, had been uttering their words of warning, the former pair to Israel and the latter to Judah. They had not been heeded, and in due course Israel was no more. But Judah lived on intact for a full century. Not surprising, thought the southerners, we have Jehovah's dwelling-place, and that can never be destroyed.

Jeremiah saw differently. After Josiah's death, idolatry and immorality came back once more into the nation's religious programme, and Jeremiah knew that this could not go unpunished. He foretold the exile, and the destruction of the Temple, and even saw beyond to the hope of a return to a new life in the land which God had promised to His people. He lived to see the events of 597 and 586, but he was a lone voice, a tragic, persecuted figure whom everyone ignored.

While Jeremiah stayed on in Palestine, Ezekiel had gone with the first batch of exiles into Babylonia. There they lived in a sort of internment camp, but as time went on they were allowed limited freedom of movement and were able to build houses and to cultivate the ground. Some became so involved in commerce that they grew rich and would not return to their native land when at last they could. But to begin with they were a community numbed with the shock of their deportation. They felt as if God had deserted them. Ezekiel needed to tell them over and over again that it was their sins that had brought this calamity upon them. Moreover, the sins of Jerusalem were such that still greater punishment was to follow, but one day God would restore the exiles to their land and make them new people with a new heart and a new spirit.

Meanwhile the religious needs of the thousands of exiles had to be faced. With no Temple, animal sacrifices were impossible (which was not a bad thing, because they had become so infected with idolatry that they were best abandoned for a while). Instead, stress was laid on the sabbath as a day of worship, on circumcision as the distinctive sign which marked them off from their Babylonian neighbours, on open-air meetings for confession, prayer and the reading of the Law, and on smaller house-meetings for instruction in the Law. So was formed the religious tradition which eventually grew into the Jewish religion as we know it today, supported by the four pillars of synagogue, scriptures, sabbath and circumcision.

The end of the Babylonian empire was announced by the writing on the wall of Belshazzar's palace, as described in the memorable passage in Daniel chapter 5. This too was the end of the Exile. In 538 B.C., Cyrus of Persia entered Babylon and proclaimed freedom to all enslaved peoples. This was a shrewd political move because it ensured good-will for his own regime throughout his newly-won empire. He even went so far as to restore to the Jews the Temple treasures which Nebuchadnezzar had looted from Jerusalem. Two years later, the first group of exiles made the long journey back to Jerusalem under the leadership of Zerubbabel.

At first, the rebuilding of the Temple was begun with enthusiasm as funds and materials came steadily in. Within months the new foundations were ready, but then opposition delayed the work. It came from the Samaritans and from the people who had settled in Judah during the years of exile. Enthusiasm waned, and more than ten years later the prophets Haggai and Zechariah had to take up the matter and exhort the people to set to again. This time they were more successful, and in 515 B.C., the second Temple was dedicated amid great rejoicing.

□ After the Exile

Very little is known about the period which followed the return from exile. The only information which the Bible gives us is contained in the little prophecies of Haggai and Zechariah, which we have already referred to, and in the books of Ezra and Nehemiah. Before we look more closely at them, however, we must not forget to notice the tremendous importance in the thought of the Old Testament which was given to the historical event of the return.

The prophets of the previous two centuries had many a time forecast that one day Judah's sins would catch up with her, and, like her northern neighbour Israel, she would be overrun and her people scattered to the four corners of the earth. At the same time they had sometimes added that one day God in His faithfulness would bring them back to their native land by a deliverance quite as miraculous as the crossing of the Red Sea in the days of Moses.

"I will be found of you, saith the Lord: and I will turn away your captivity, and I will gather you from all the nations, and from all the places whither I have driven you, saith the Lord; and I will bring you again into the place whence I caused you to be carried away captive (Jeremiah 29: 14).

"Awake, awake, put on strength,
O arm of the Lord;
awake, as in days of old,
the generations of long ago . . .
Was it not thou that didst dry up the sea,
the waters of the great deep;
that didst make the depths of the sea a way
for the redeemed to pass over?
And the ransomed of the Lord shall return,
and come to Zion with singing . . ."
(Isaiah 51: 9 ff. (R.S.V.))

Nothing less than a new age was expected now that the exiles had come back to their beloved Jerusalem, but the setbacks and opposition they had to face quickly brought them down to earth. We have already seen that Haggai and Zechariah had to work hard to keep the people at the job of rebuilding and even in the midst of the general pleasure in its eventual completion there were the greybeards who remembered the magnificence of Solomon's Temple and shook their heads sadly at the poverty of this modern replacement.

For all that, the second Temple was recognised by Jews everywhere as their spiritual home. Since the dark days of exile, Jews far from home had begun to turn towards Jerusalem whenever they said their prayers (as Daniel did, 6: 10), and this practice grew. Many Jews never returned to Jerusalem: some stayed in Babylon and prospered there; many more had fled to Egypt after 586 (among them the unwilling Jeremiah) and established colonies there. In all sorts of places they were dispersed abroad; but their links were always with Jerusalem. From the famous papyri of Elephantine in Lower Egypt we have evidence of how a colony of Jews maintained their religious life, with their own temple to Jehovah, but still closely in touch with the High Priest in Jerusalem.

For years after 515 B.C., there was a steady trickle of Jews returning home and with them came Ezra the Scribe who made the journey in 458 B.C. He was sent at the command of the Persian king Artaxerxes, and with generous funds at his disposal, to organise the Jewish community and to establish the Temple worship according to the Mosaic Law. Thirteen years later, Nehemiah was permitted to go up to Jerusalem, also with the king's blessing, and he made it his particular responsibility to see that the city around the Temple was properly fortified and that the ruined walls were rebuilt. This was a political, even a military, move to some people and it was only achieved against great opposition from Sanballat, the Samaritan leader.

42

Once it was done, Ezra was called upon to proclaim the Law to the people, the ancient Feast of Tabernacles was revived, and the people entered into a covenant to obey the Law of Moses and to maintain their racial and religious purity. From this time onwards, the religion of the Jews became primarily a religion of birth and of race, so that today the only true Jew is the man who is born a Jew.

Four hundred more years were to elapse before the coming of Jesus Christ to bring in the new age of the New Testament. These were important years for the formation of Jewish beliefs, the development of religious pressure-groups like the Pharisees and Sadducees, the teachings of the rabbis, and the influence of Greek culture and philosophy upon the religion of the Jews. All this, however, is more a matter for New Testament background, and is not our present concern, so we shall close the story here and turn now to give a closer look at the books of the Old Testament and what they contain.

4 THE THIRTY-NINE BOOKS

If you open your Bible at the contents page, you will find the list of the thirty-nine books of the Old Testament. Speaking very roughly, they consist first of seventeen books which are history, then five books which are poetry, then a further seventeen books which are prophecy.

The history books can be further divided into five books of Moses and twelve others; and the prophecy books can be divided into five major and twelve minor prophets. Thus we have a scheme of: $(5 + 12) + 5 + (5 + 12) = 39$.

Or, written in full, we have:

Genesis	Joshua	2 Kings	
Exodus	Judges	1 Chronicles	
Leviticus +	Ruth	2 Chronicles	History
Numbers	1 Samuel	Ezra	
Deuteronomy	2 Samuel	Nehemiah	
	1 Kings	Esther	

Job			
Psalms			
Proverbs			} Poetry
Ecclesiastes			
Song of Solomon			

Isaiah	Hosea	Nahum	
Jeremiah	Joel	Habakkuk	
Lamentations +	Amos	Zephaniah	
Ezekiel	Obadiah	Haggai	} Prophecy
Daniel	Jonah	Zechariah	
	Micah	Malachi	

Now we can look at the three sections in greater detail. But because the first five books are so important, we shall give them an additional section at the beginning.

☐ **1. The Law**

The five books of Moses, the Pentateuch, were always thought by the Jews to be particularly inspired and they were given prominence over the rest of the Old Testament. There were even some, like the Sadducees in our Lord's day, who felt that the books of Moses were the only inspired books. So when Jesus tried to convince them of the truth of the resurrection (which they did not believe in) He had to use the Pentateuch to prove it, and you can read how He did it in Mark 12: 18–27.

We do not believe that one part of the Bible is more inspired than the rest. The whole Bible is inspired, or

God-breathed, and you cannot over-emphasise certain books or chapters without getting into trouble. Even though we may have our favourite passages or find certain books more helpful spiritually, the whole Book is God's revelation, and we are not permitted to prune it or play with it. We must put ourselves under the judgment of the Bible and not the Bible under the judgment of ourselves.

The Pentateuch was called the Torah, the Law. It contained the Ten Commandments and the early laws given by Moses. It is fundamental to the whole of the Old Testament.

The story it tells is from the beginning of the world up to the death of Moses. No one, incidentally, thinks that Moses wrote about his own death, but most of the Pentateuch has come down to us substantially from Moses' day.

Genesis is the book of beginnings. The first eleven chapters tell of the creation of the world, of the first people in it, the first sin, the first murder, the first great act of judgment in the Flood, the beginnings of language and so on. Everything is in its infancy.

Modern readers often look at these chapters and dismiss them as mere legends. Genesis 1 to 11 used to be the battleground for all the old science versus the Bible conflicts. Today thoughtful people no longer see a conflict, they see instead some of the most profound writings in the whole of the Old Testament.

There are two ways of understanding these chapters. Either they can be taken as literal fact, not of course written in scientific language but accurate all the same.

Or they can be taken as parables in which the truth is wrapped up in picture language. It is well to remember that earnest Christians hold both of these views. What is fundamental, however, is that these chapters are to be considered as history, and they can be defended as historically trustworthy, subject though they are to differences of interpretation.

After Genesis 12 we have the family history of Abraham, Isaac, Jacob and Joseph—a fascinating story of faith and folly, obedience and disobedience, courage and perversity. The thin red line that runs through this story, as we saw in the last chapter, is God's promise to bless the seed of Abraham, and His protection of them through all adversities, even to the extent of allowing Joseph to be sold into slavery in Egypt so that he could later be the means of saving his family in the years of famine.

Exodus is the book of deliverance. It begins with the life story of Moses, brought up in Pharaoh's palace, called by God at the burning bush, challenging Pharaoh to let His people go free and eventually leading them through the miraculous crossing of the Red Sea into the wilderness of the Sinai peninsula. The second part of the book tells of the revelation at Mount Sinai. The giving of the Ten Commandments is followed by three chapters of laws. Then follow in great detail the instructions for the building of the Ark of testimony, the Tabernacle in which it is to be housed and all the equipment which is to surround it, the clothing of the priests and the sacrifices they are to offer.

At first reading all this detail may seem boring and totally irrelevant. But when you read it, remember that the children of Israel had no Bible or Church through which to know the God they were to worship: all they were given was this great visual-aid, the Tabernacle, and every detail of its construction, appearance and ceremonial was intended to teach the worshippers something about the God they served. So when you read about it, keep asking yourself questions like, 'What would this have meant to the children of Israel when they went to worship God? Why were all the fittings made only of the finest and costliest materials? Why was it that nobody was allowed to go into the holy of holies? Why was it so important that every little detail had to be just so?' You will soon realise that the answers to questions like these tell you a great deal about what the God of the Israelites was like and what He expected of His people.

Leviticus is Latin for 'the Levitical book', or the book of the priests. It consists mainly of instructions given to Moses regarding the rituals of Israelite life and worship. There is very little narrative, and the book ends where it began, with the Israelites still encamped at the foot of Mount Sinai.

Once again the ritual laws are intended to teach something positive, and should be read in that light. They are not binding on Christians, but of course the moral laws are, unless they have been superseded or re-applied by the New Testament.

Much of Leviticus deals with the sacrifices and

offerings which were required of the children of Israel (chapters 1 to 7). This is tremendously important for the Christian reader because it helps him to understand the Jewish custom of sacrifice which was regularly performed in Jesus' day and which Jesus Himself thought of in relation to His death. The New Testament constantly describes His death as a *sacrifice* for sin and only in the light of Leviticus 1 to 7 can we understand fully the meaning of the Cross. We shall refer to this again in chapter five.

Numbers begins, as you would expect, with the numbering of the tribes, but only for four chapters. The book continues with still more legislation and with practical arrangements for the service of the Tabernacle, but from chapter 10 v. 11 onwards the narrative is taken up again as the tribes prepare to move towards the promised land.

At this stage the Israelites came to a kind of cross-roads. They sent twelve spies to survey the land of Canaan and they came back with such a gloomy story about the strength of the inhabitants of the land that the Israelites lost heart and wished they had never left Egypt. Two of the twelve, however, were men of faith and they were confident that they could over-come the Canaanites in the power of God. Their names were Caleb and Joshua. But two lone voices against the chicken-hearted multitude could do little and they were shouted down and nearly lynched.

Then God intervened and, through Moses, pronounced His judgment on the people: not one of them would ever set foot in the promised land, except for Caleb and Joshua. As the people had rejected God's good provision of a national home, He was rejecting them. So the Israelites wandered in the wilderness for forty years and a new generation was born.

Numbers tells a sorry story of cowardice, stupidity and defeat. Yet through it all God remains faithful to His promise that one day He will lead His people into the land flowing with milk and honey.

Deuteronomy means 'the second law' or 'the law repeated', and consists mainly of addresses given by Moses to the people. In them he traces the history of their wanderings since Sinai, reminds them of the commandments given to them there, and introduces a large collection of further laws which were intended to have special reference to their life in the land of Canaan. The book concludes with a solemn covenant which he calls upon the people to make, binding them to the service of the Lord their God.

Finally, Moses gives his blessing to the tribes (chapter 33) and, viewing the promised land from the top of Mount Pisgah, he dies within sight of Canaan but is never allowed to set foot upon it himself. This privilege was reserved for his able successor, Joshua.

☐ **2. The Histories**

The Book of Joshua continues the story from the death of Moses at the end of Deuteronomy. Throughout it is a book of victory. And as with all victories in the spiritual life, it begins with dedication. Joshua's first act was to listen to the voice of the

Lord commanding him to follow in the ways of Moses.

"Be strong and very courageous, being careful to do according to all the law which Moses my servant commanded you . . . This book of the law shall not depart out of your mouth, but you shall meditate on it day and night, that you may be careful to do according to all that is written in it; for then you shall make your way prosperous, and then you shall have good success" (Joshua 1: 7, 8).

Then he began to plan for the invasion of Canaan. At every step he was successful—in the crossing of the river Jordan, the capture of Jericho and his lightning military operations against the strategic cities of Canaan. Once he failed tragically, at Ai. This was because of the greed of Achan, one of his soldiers, who tried to keep for himself part of the spoil from Jericho instead of letting it be offered to God. The penalty for this was severe: Achan and everything and everybody who were infected by his disobedience had to be rooted out and destroyed. No more devastating illustration could be given of the message of Joshua, that whereas complete dedication brings complete victory, defective dedication ends in disaster.

This was the principle that God applied to the people of Canaan. He insisted that none of them was to be left alive to infect the Israelites with their depraved religious practices. We in our spirit of Christian tolerance are inclined to think this was a bit hard on them, but when we realise that the religion of Canaan was a fertility religion, that is to say, a religion centred on sex, with sexual symbols and organised prostitution at every temple or 'high place', we can see why it had to be stamped out ruthlessly if the pure faith of Jehovah the God of Israel was not to be swamped.

The second half of this book tells how the land was to be divided up among the twelve tribes of Israel. To make any sense of this you need to have a Bible atlas beside you, and even then it will be heavy-going. The Biblical archaeologist, however, finds this fascinating territory to assist his researches!

The book ends with the dedication of the people, as Joshua makes a final covenant with them at Shechem and they cry out to him, "The Lord our God we will serve, and his voice we will obey" (Joshua 24: 24).

The Book of Judges. We do not have to read far before we find that the individual tribes "did not wholly drive out the Canaanites" from the areas allotted to them, and it was their failure at this point which brought about the chaos and confusion reflected in the book of Judges. Whoever it was who wrote the book (and none of the history books give much of a clue as to who wrote them) was at pains to point out that history repeated itself. A certain pattern of history could be seen again and again in the life of Israel under the Judges.

This pattern is described in chapter 2: 11–23. It consisted of five stages:

1. The people of Israel did what was evil in the sight of the Lord; they forsook the Lord and served

Baal, the god of the Canaanites, and went after other gods.

2. The Lord's anger came upon Israel and He gave them up to be ravaged by some foreign power—Moabites, Midianites, Ammonites, Philistines, etc.

3. Then the Lord had pity on His people's sufferings and raised up Judges to deliver them.

4. The Judges were given victory and success against their foes.

5. But when the Judges died the people reverted to their sinful, idolatrous ways . . . and so the pattern began all over again.

This pattern of sin, judgment, mercy, salvation and backsliding is worked out in some detail in the stories of Gideon and Samson, but it underlies the whole of the book including the careers of the less famous Judges.

The book concludes with an appendix to illustrate the moral and religious decline of the times (chapters 17 to 21). Two incidents are described in detail to show the depths of sin to which the people had sunk: falsehood, murder, homosexuality, rape, civil war and mass abduction were some of the results of men going their own way and not God's way. The key verse, repeated twice in these chapters, tells the tale: "Every man did what was right in his own eyes."

Ruth follows on as a most delightful contrast. The events which it describes took place in the days of the Judges, but instead of dealing with moral decay this little book tells the story of the loyalty of Ruth the Moabitess to her mother-in-law, Naomi. Ruth's devotion is rewarded by another act of loyalty, this time on the part of Naomi's kinsman, Boaz, who fulfils his family responsibilities by marrying Ruth and making a home for her. The importance of the story is that this union of Ruth and Boaz produced in the third generation the great king David, and thence "great David's greater Son".

1 and 2 Samuel are really one book and between them cover a period of a hundred years, from c. 1050 to 950 B.C. The story is centred on three characters, the lives of Samuel, Saul and David, and contains some of the most readable 'adventure-stories' in the whole of the Bible.

It is easy to miss the real point of the book in the sheer interest of the contents. From the political point of view it represents the transition from a theocracy to a monarchy, i.e., from the rule of God (through His servant the priest or prophet) to the rule of one man as king. This is represented very much as a second best, and the failure of Saul only serves to underline this judgment. By David's time, however, the stigma of the monarchy had died away, and he was not penalised on this account.

More personally, however, we have here the parallel descriptions of two men, both from relatively humble origins, who had greatness thrust upon them. Saul's head was turned by his promotion from being a tribal chieftain to being head of state. David, however, showed that he could wear his honours well, and was "a man after the Lord's own heart". Significantly, his character is not whitewashed in any way. He was capable of sins like revenge and lust, but he was also capable of great heroism, affection, courage and sensitivity.

One of the last acts recorded of David was his sin in numbering the people. It is not easy to say what the sin was in holding such a census. Possibly it was a completely unprofitable counting of heads, and it was condemned for that reason; more probably, the result of the census was to elevate David's heart and it was condemned for its consequences. God punished the people with a pestilence which was only halted when David built an altar on the threshing-floor of Araunah the Jebusite. His purchase of the land surrounding the altar was not only a mark of penitence but it had a long-term significance in providing the ground on which his son could later build the Temple. The incident illustrates clearly the way in which sin, repentance and ultimate blessing so often marked David's spiritual experience.

1 and 2 Kings are also a single book with a very artificial and unnatural division. The Greek Bible actually regards Samuel and Kings as one continuous history and numbers the books 1, 2, 3 and 4 Kings, but this is unnecessary because the two books were completed at different times.

The period of history covered by Kings is about four hundred years. It begins with the closing years of David's reign and ends with Jehoiachin's release from captivity in Babylon in 562 B.C. The treatment of the period is not uniform. The first eleven chapters are devoted to Solomon's reign and achievements covering only forty years; the next twenty-eight chapters (to 2 Kings 17) tell the story of the divided kingdoms from 930 B.C. to Israel's fall in 722; and the last eight chapters complete the history of Judah from then until the exile.

The most noticeable thing about the book is the concentration given to two particular periods of the history, the reign of Solomon and the prophetic ministry of Elijah and Elisha. The importance of the first is obvious, because Solomon was as great in his way as David his father. The two prophets of Israel, however, represented the great northern resistance movement against the corrupting influences of Ahab and Baal-religion. This has been described as a "spiritually crucial epoch which saw an outburst of miraculous power such as had not occurred since the time of the Exodus".

A further matter for comment is the religious judgment which the writer of Kings makes on every king as he is mentioned. However briefly his reign may be recorded, no king gets away without a reference to whether he did that which was good, or more usually that which was evil, in the sight of the Lord.

1 and 2 Chronicles cover much the same ground as the histories of Samuel and Kings, but they are intended to supplement them by retelling the story from a religious standpoint. The Chronicler is interested mainly in the Temple and its institutions, so Solomon gets full treatment as its builder, and David's life-story is limited to those aspects which have a bearing on religious worship. All this is preceded by an enormous genealogy, or family tree, tracing David's line right back from Adam.

Because the Chronicler is only interested in the Temple, he studiously ignores anything that happened in the northern kingdom of Israel, but it is well worth while comparing the accounts of southern kings in both Kings and Chronicles to see how differently the same reign is treated. Best of all, Chronicles includes some pearls of devotion in such passages as the prayer of David at the great Gift Day of the Temple Building Fund (1 Chronicles 29), and the prayer of Solomon at the eventual dedication of the Temple (2 Chronicles 6).

Ezra and Nehemiah are closely connected with 1 and 2 Chronicles, and all four books are sometimes thought of as sections of one large work. Certainly they all reflect the same outlook, and may well have been compiled by the same man, though Ezra and Nehemiah contain large sections of personal memoirs written by the two men themselves. Because of these eye-witness accounts, the books have an added interest for the reader.

The writer gives great prominence to the opposition that faced the builders, both of the Temple and of the city walls, and the sections dealing with the way in which opposition was successfully resisted give the books their enduring message. Add to them the spirit of prayer and personal devotion of the two main characters, and it is not surprising that these two little histories have held a special place in the hearts of Christian readers.

If ever you find yourself really up against it, facing

hostility or persecution for the service of Christ, turn back to Ezra and Nehemiah, especially Nehemiah 4 to 6, and remind yourself how these men of old fought and worked, prayed and trusted, and finally won the day. You'll never lose heart again!

Esther has the distinction of being the only book in the Bible in which God is never mentioned. The story is an exciting incident from Persian times, telling of the deliverance of the Jews in Persia from an anti-Semitic plot to massacre them. The two heroes, the Jewish Queen Esther, and her cousin Mordecai, are still commemorated in the annual feast of Purim, and we must suppose that the book was included in Hebrew scripture because of its connection with this feast. Without using God's name, it nevertheless tells a remarkable story of God's protection of His people, and shows how a lonely believer in a key position can be used by God to do great things for Him.

□ 3. *The Poetry*

The Book of Job deals with one of the oldest problems in religion, the problem of suffering. The poem is introduced by an encounter in heaven between God and Satan, as a result of which Satan is allowed to plague Job with almost every evil short of taking his life. However, it is soon clear that Job's suffering is only partly his actual bodily pain and mental grief; his real anguish comes from not being able to understand why God has allowed an innocent man like him to suffer so much.

His three friends knew the answer, so they thought. Job *must* have been more wicked than he admitted and that was why he suffered. Job on the other hand clung to his innocence, and went through torment.

The tantalising thing about the Book of Job is that the problem does not appear to be answered; it is merely discussed. Job's faith rises to enormous heights, as in his great affirmation, "I know that my redeemer liveth", but the next moment he is in the doldrums again. The answer however does come, in a round-about way. God finally speaks out (38 to 41) and very strangely proceeds to describe the wonders of His handiwork, in particular the hippopotamus and the crocodile! Somehow this reminder of the greatness of God as seen in creation satisfies Job and he admits his own creatureliness, and cries out: "I have heard of thee by the hearing of the ear: but now mine eye seeth thee. Wherefore I abhor myself, and repent in dust and ashes" (42: 5, 6).

The answer to Job's dilemma is not therefore explained in the way that he was wanting, but as he sees what a great God it is that he serves, he finds his problems evaporating into comparative insignificance. It is an answer which does not satisfy the pure philosopher, and writers still try to grapple with the question of evil and suffering in God's world. But in terms of practical living it is surely the greatest answer that has ever been produced.

The Psalms are the hymn-book of the Bible. In a hundred and fifty poems they give us every mood of the life of the believer and express penitence and praise, fear and faith, thanksgiving and assurance. There is no experience which cannot be matched by the words of one or other of the psalms. This is because they were composed in moments of spiritual crisis, and they were regularly used in the worship of the Jewish Temple at appropriate occasions—fasts, festivals, anniversaries, national days of prayer and so on.

Some of the psalms are national, where everything is in the plural and vast crowds are pictured at prayer; others are deeply personal, fit only to be muttered silently as the worshipper tries to express repentance for his sin, or pleads for help and deliverance from some besetting enemy. Others are public acts of thanksgiving, when a man goes up to the Temple to give thanks for a great answer to prayer, perhaps deliverance from danger or a serious illness.

It is sometimes possible to imagine the setting of some of the psalms as they might have been used at a Temple service, accompanying a sacrifice, or sung at a feast. Indeed, with a little imagination, you can even see a few psalms as liturgies, with one line or stanza being said by the high priest, the next by the Temple singers, the next by the thankful offerer, and a chorus by everybody.

For the Christian, however, the important thing is to become familiar with the psalms, and you can then draw up your own list of which psalms to turn to in a given situation, e.g., when tired, depressed, thankful, repentant, afraid, etc. The psalms are intended first and foremost to be used as a regular feature of one's devotional life.

Some people are worried by the so-called imprecatory psalms where the psalmist wishes all sorts of unpleasant things upon evil-doers, which would not be very suitable as Christian prayers. This of course is true, and some psalms are not ideally suited for public worship. The point of these psalms is that the psalmist had such a strong concern for God's honour, that his blood boiled at the disobedience of the wicked, and their blatant scoffing at God's holiness. The way he expressed his ardour might have been pretty basic, but at least it was thoroughly sincere, and we could learn something of that holy zeal ourselves. It is not far from there to the cry "the zeal of thine house has eaten me up", which came into the disciples' minds as they watched our Lord driving out the money-changers from the Temple (John 2: 17).

It is impossible to read the psalms without being struck first by the great spiritual stature of David, who was responsible for many of these beautiful compositions, and also by the spiritual wealth of the generations of Old Testament worshippers who used them. It is a great heritage that has been handed down to the Christian Church and we will benefit immeasurably the more we learn to make it our own.

The best way to start is to read one a day for five months, and by that time you should be well on the way to knowing how best to use them in your own daily prayers.

Proverbs. We normally think that there were only two classes of religious leader in Old Testament days, the prophets and the priests. There was, however, a third, called by Jeremiah (18: 18) "the wise", and classed with the other two. They were a class of philosophers who were found throughout the Middle East and they have left behind their writings in Egypt, Babylonia and elsewhere. In Israel, 'wisdom' was highly regarded, and individuals like Samson (with his famous riddle, Judges 14), Solomon and Hezekiah were exponents of the art.

The wise men produced crisp, popular sayings which contained sound sense for daily living, and also tried to plumb the depths of some of the real problems of life. The Book of Job is an example of the latter, and Proverbs is a collection of the former.

Many of the proverbs are unrelated to each other, or grouped together only roughly, so they do not make easy consecutive reading. Their chief virtue is that as a number are read, the odd one stands out for its aptness to one's particular situation. A recent commentator has described Proverbs as "a book which seldom takes you to church . . . Its function . . . is to put godliness into working clothes". This is well said, and the reader will find here no empty religious talk, but thrusting words about matters of practical Christianity, e.g., are you too talkative? what are you like when you get up in the morning? can you keep a confidence? how do you treat your parents? how are you to choose a wife? All this sound sense springs from God. "The fear of the Lord is the beginning of wisdom: and the knowledge of the Holy One is understanding". There are many who never attain to it: they are lazy, troublesome, selfish, spoilt, or ensnared by immoral women. The reader is warned against these and many other pitfalls. The ideal wife is described in chapter 31 as an example of industry, business ability and faithfulness, but again it is her religion that counts most. "Charm is deceitful and beauty is vain: but a woman who fears the Lord shall be praised."

Ecclesiastes, or the Book of the Preacher, is an attempt to find out the meaning of life. The writer asks questions and offers answers about the purpose of existence. The book continually see-saws between the questions, which are usually put as statements about the futility of life—"vanity of vanities, saith the preacher: all is vanity"—and the answers, which express the need to live a godly life if only because one day we will have to render an account to God.

Within this framework there is much that the reader is intended to reject because it represents the musing of the natural man, but there is much also that is the distinctive message of the book. These parts (the answers given by the author) teach the need for remembering God while one is still young, living day by day in faith and contentment, leaving the future in God's hands, and using every opportunity that life affords, because when old age and death come, it will be too late.

The Song of Solomon is one of the most beautiful love songs that has ever been written. It illustrates the richness of human love and helps the Christian to look beyond to an even greater love that is only to be found in Christ. It found its place in the Hebrew

Bible, and thence in our own, simply because it was thought to be a picture of God's gracious dealings with His people, and commentators (both Jewish and Christian) have vied with each other in producing more and more highly spiritualised interpretations. In origin, however, it was not a religious poem, but a poem of love, and its place in the Bible is a healthy reminder that religion and human love are not incompatible.

□ 4. The Prophets

As children we were taught that the prophet is not someone who fore-tells, but who 'forth-tells'. That is to say, he is a spokesman for today, rather than for tomorrow or for the distant future. The prophets of the Old Testament were men who could receive messages from God and speak them out to His people. As a result the genuine ones were often unpopular, or unheeded, and there arose a class of men who called themselves prophets, but who spoke less demandingly. These were the false prophets who spoke peace when there was no peace, and who gave comforting messages regardless of the truth.

The true prophets therefore had two forces to contend with, the stubbornness of the people and the deceitfulness of their own colleagues. Despite this, however, some exercised great national influence and not all were doomed to be like Jeremiah, who was cruelly persecuted for his preaching.

The books of the writing prophets are really collections of prophecies, many of them undated and difficult to place in a historical context. Usually they refer to their own time, but occasionally they foretell the certainty of God's judgment or the prospect of renewed blessing, and once in a while they speak greater than they know and make some statement which has a remarkable reference to the coming of Christ. This, however, is the exception and not the rule.

Really, the prophets were religious commentators. Knowing the standards of God they applied them to the political, social and religious scene with devastating directness. Sometimes their messages were received in a vision or when they were in a kind of trance, but more often they were careful compositions which came from an inner compulsion to say something about a given situation or incident. Their utterances were later recorded, probably by their disciples, and the resulting collections are as we have them.

Isaiah was one of the quartet of eighth-century prophets with Amos, Hosea and Micah. He was a southerner and a man who was closely mixed up with the life of the court. He therefore had the ear of the kings under whom he served; Uzziah, Jotham, Ahaz and Hezekiah. It is gratifying to note, according to 2 Kings, that all but Ahaz did that which was right in the eyes of the Lord.

His prophecy covered the years from 740–700 B.C., and so he saw the overthrow of Samaria, the northern capital, by the Assyrians in 722. His great burden was the holiness of the Lord, a message which was burned into him at his call in chapter 6, "in the year that king Uzziah died". It may not be a coincidence that Uzziah had died a leper, through having flouted the holiness of God, and the circumstances of this tragedy may have been uppermost in Isaiah's mind when his vision came to him. (For the story of this read 2 Chronicles 26: 16–21).

Because the Lord was a holy God two things followed. First, the sins of God's people had to be publicly denounced, as committed against a God who was of purer eyes than to behold iniquity. At the same time it meant that God was too faithful to break the holy covenant which He had made with His people. So God's holiness brought about punishment for sin, *and* the assurance of salvation.

The punishment was seen by Isaiah mostly in terms of an invasion by an enemy and the obvious quarter that this would come from was Assyria. The Assyrian armies did in fact invade Judaea in Hezekiah's day, but the people were given a stay of execution and the punishment did not finally fall until a century later when the Babylonians under Nebuchadnezzar brought Jerusalem to her knees, as Isaiah had foreseen (39: 6).

The message of salvation comes out most fully in chapters 40 to 66. These chapters need to be read in the light of the background of the Babylonian exile. They enlarge on the Holy God's faithfulness to His people in bringing them back to their own land. They describe the joy of the returning exiles and look forward with hope to the new age which will dawn. All through the book Isaiah strikes this note of the golden age of the future. The Messiah is seen as the Prince of Peace in an age when wild animals will live peacefully together. He will be of the family of David and will judge the people righteously.

Later, however, he is described in a group of four poems, known as the Servant Songs (42: 1–7; 49: 1–6; 50: 4–11; 52: 13 to 53: 12), as the servant of the Lord who suffers for the sins of His people. Here we reach the high point of Isaiah's prophecy, and some of the most clear-cut forecasts of the ministry and death of Christ. It is not surprising that Isaiah has been called the Evangelist of the Old Testament.

Jeremiah is popularly thought of as the prophet of gloom. If a person is called a Jeremiah, it means that he is miserable, heartless, and always looking on the black side of things. The name probably arises from the little book he wrote rather unfortunately called Lamentations, but in fact Jeremiah was far from being like his popular image. True he was a fierce preacher of judgment, but it was always mingled with hope. He was misunderstood and disliked, but only because he was faithful to his message and it was an unpopular message. Here was clearly a case of the false prophets being approved because their messages were easy, and the lone voice of truth being rejected and persecuted.

The situation was roughly this. About 600 B.C., Nebuchadnezzar and the Babylonian armies, having crushed the Egyptians in battle at Carchemish, looked set to overrun Judah and Jerusalem. King Jehoiachin's policy wavered between allying himself with Egypt or with Babylon. Jeremiah said: "Submit to the

Babylonians." Had his advice been followed, Judah could have remained subject to Nebuchadnezzar and kept Jerusalem and the Temple intact, but the rash patriotism of the people thought otherwise, and first Jehoiakim and later Zedekiah rebelled and suffered the consequences. Jeremiah endured the eighteen-months siege of Jerusalem which ended in Zedekiah's capture and the sack of the city.

Inevitably Jeremiah's message sounded treacherous, or at best cowardly, to his fellow-Jews. They very nearly took his life on more than one occasion, and to make matters worse Nebuchadnezzar gave him V.I.P. treatment after the siege was ended! Were it not for Jeremiah's patent sincerity and the obvious rightness of the message he preached, he could easily have been branded as a traitor and not as the patriot that he was.

The tragedy of Jeremiah is not merely that he was doomed to be ignored, but that he was of a sensitive disposition and could scarcely bear the treatment he had to endure. His stern messages came from a heart that loved Judah deeply, and it nearly broke his heart that the people reacted as they did.

Yet he was sure that the exile would end—seventy years in all he gave it. Then at last, God would restore His people—not only to their old land, but with a new heart. The old stubbornness would be gone: instead they would have God's Law written within their hearts, and would be obedient to His commandments. Only part of this prophecy was fulfilled in the return from exile: the remainder took another six hundred years to be fulfilled, when the Holy Spirit was given to the Church at Pentecost.

In the five *Lamentations of Jeremiah* which are added as a kind of supplement to the main work, the prophet looks at the ashes of the stricken city of Jerusalem and bewails its loss, in particular because its destruction was avoidable. He sees it as the logical result of defying God's laws, but he remembers also God's unfailing love, and tenderly calls on his people to repent and acknowledge their sins.

"Why dost thou forget us for ever, why dost
thou so long forsake us?
Restore us to thyself, O Lord, that we
may be restored!" (Lamentations 5: 20 f.).

Ezekiel was one of those taken into captivity to Babylon with the first deportation in 597 B.C., and it was only while he was in captivity that he received his call to be a spokesman for God to his fellow-exiles. He had been brought up in a priestly family and was well-versed in Jewish symbolism, which he often used in his messages, illustrating them with a rough drawing or a symbolical action.

The first half of his ministry he was preparing the exiled Jews for the eventual destruction of the Temple which he knew must take place as a judgment on Jerusalem's sins. It was incredible to them that a prophet of Jehovah should speak like this about Jehovah's Temple, because to them the existence of God was bound up with the permanence of His dwelling-place. Even after all his warnings the exiles were thunderstruck when the news eventually arrived (33: 21), and from then on Ezekiel's message became one of comfort, restoration and hope.

While to many readers the most baffling part of Ezekiel's prophecy is his vision of the chariot-throne of God in chapters 1 and 10, where he tries to describe the indescribable, the most reassuring chapter is the vision of the valley of dry bones (37), which tells of the Holy Spirit's ability to make dead men live. The concluding section of the book (chapters 40 to 48) outlines the plan for a Temple that was to be built in the restored Jerusalem, a design that was probably never intended to be taken too literally, for its language at times topples over into pure symbolism rather like the description of heaven in the Book of the Revelation.

It is rather surprising that Ezekiel nowhere makes any reference to his contemporary Jeremiah. True, they were separated by hundreds of miles, but you cannot read his book without realising how much he has borrowed, even at that great distance, from the lonely prophet in Jerusalem. Perhaps you could say that Ezekiel's prophecy is the one proof that Jeremiah's words did not fall on completely deaf ears.

Daniel, too, lived during the same period of exile, but he was early raised to high office in the kingdom of Babylonia. The book which bears his name consists of a series of adventures, followed by a series of visions about the future. The adventures are remarkable stories demonstrating the truth that God honours those who honour Him, whether it is a matter of keeping to simple food instead of eating the king's dainties, or of not bowing down to any god but the God of Israel. In several of them, Daniel shows that God had equipped him with special ability in interpreting dreams and visions, an art which was highly prized by the Babylonians, and the four visions which occupy the last six chapters give evidence of this supernatural gift. The visions are prophetic, and although it is by no means agreed how they should be interpreted, it is fairly clear that they describe subsequent world-empires culminating in the kingdom of the saints.

Daniel lived through the dying years of the Babylonian empire of Nebuchadnezzar and seems to have retained his influence under the rule of the early Persian emperors as well. His book is a monument to the courage of men who would not lower their standards whatever pressure they underwent, and at the same time it lifts a corner of the veil that covers the events of the last days to give us some idea of what is to come, even though we shall never know in advance when it will be.

The Minor Prophets, as Dr. Campbell Morgan wrote, "are minor in no sense save that of bulk". Originally regarded as one book, they are nevertheless a collection of books arranged in no historical order for the simple reason that several of the books cannot be dated with any certainty. We shall, therefore, deal with them in groups. The first are the three prophets of the eighth century B.C.

71

1. *Amos, Hosea and Micah*

Amos was a countryman from Tekoa in the Judaean hills, who frequently visited Bethel in the north where the kings of Israel had established the shrine with the golden calf. He did not profess to be a prophet but he could not contain his feelings and he spoke up against the sins of the people of Israel. His great theme was the judgment of God, which was not, as his hearers supposed, just reserved for the heathen round about, but was upon those who knew the truth and failed to follow it.

"You only have I known of all the families of the earth; therefore will I punish you for all your iniquities" (Amos 3: 2).

Hosea's message was based on his own tragic marriage with the faithless Gomer. He then pictures God's love for His people as the love of a husband for a faithless wife, a love which would never fail but would pursue and woo her until he had brought her back to himself. "Thy love," says Hosea to Israel, "is like a morning cloud" (6: 4). It lasts for a little while and then vanishes away.

If Amos speaks of judgment and Hosea of the love of God, *Micah's* message is His righteousness. From dealing with the sins of Samaria and Jerusalem, and especially of their leaders, he turns to prophesy the righteous rule of the Messiah's kingdom, including the reference to Bethlehem as the Messiah's birthplace (5: 2). He shows that in God's eyes righteousness is more important than religious observances.

"What doth the Lord require of thee, but to do

justly, and to love mercy, and to walk humbly with thy God?" (6: 8).

2. *Jonah, Nahum, Zephaniah and Habakkuk*

The story of *Jonah*'s commission to preach to Nineveh, capital of the hated Assyrians, and their subsequent repentance is known only too well. The miracle of Jonah's deliverance by the great fish and the gracious act of God in giving him a second chance to obey His call give the book a timeless quality for all those engaged in Christian service. Time and again God intervened to make sure that His servant fulfilled His appointed task. Preachers find great encouragement here!

Nahum, too, deals with Nineveh, prophesying most vividly its fall and destruction, which actually took place in 612 B.C., at the hands of the Medes and Babylonians.

Zephaniah also foretells this event (2: 13), but his main pre-occupation is with the nearness of the Day of the Lord which, as Amos taught, would involve judgment upon Jerusalem quite as much as on the heathen nations round about. But with God's judgment there would also be restoration and salvation.

Habakkuk moves on to the Babylonian, or Chaldean, period at the end of the seventh century B.C., and faces up to the problem of how a holy God like Jehovah can use such a barbaric nation as the Chaldeans to be His instrument in inflicting punishment upon His people. The prophet's answer (2: 4) is that the sinner never goes unpunished, but that "the just shall live by his faith".

3. *Obadiah, Joel, Haggai, Zechariah, Malachi*

Obadiah is a brief prophecy concerning the Edomites, who had taken advantage of the misfortunes of Jerusalem at the time of its siege by invading Judah from the south.

Joel is famous for his prophecy of the time when God would pour out His spirit upon all flesh, so manifestly fulfilled on the Day of Pentecost. *Haggai* and *Zechariah*, as we noted earlier, were the prophets who encouraged the work of rebuilding the ruined Temple after the exile in 520 B.C. Their books contain some of their prophecies relating to this, and Zechariah adds a number of chapters (9 to 14) about the coming of the Messianic King, the fountain of forgiveness which will then be opened, and the great day of the Lord.

Finally, *Malachi* brings God's last word under the old covenant: "I have loved you, says the Lord." He shows up Israel's sins: despising God's name, faithlessness to the covenant, withholding the tithes which are His due, speaking against Him. And then right at the end he foretells the coming of the second Elijah, John the Baptist, who would be God's messenger to usher in the Christ of the new covenant.

5 THE OVERALL MESSAGE

As Christians, our main concern in reading the Bible is to find out what God is saying to us through it. So we conclude our survey of the Old Testament by looking more closely at its message. There are two sides to this: there is the general, over-all message, and the personal, specific message. The first is what God says to every generation and is what we are now interested in. The second is what God may say to you through a particular passage at a particular time when you are reading your Bible in an attitude of prayer, and that is your private concern which we cannot deal with here—except to say that you must always be ready for God to do that for you.

☐ The Covenant

The word 'testament' means 'covenant' or 'agreement'. So the Old Testament is the story of the old agreement which God made with His people, Israel. This agreement is set against a background of two fundamental facts:

1. *God created all things*

There was nothing in the universe for which He was not ultimately responsible. There was no territory where another deity, devil or demon held sway. Genesis chapter 1 tells this magnificently. All was carefully ordered out of the formless chaos. The first act of God was to bring light to the darkness. Then He divided and marked off the boundaries of things: the heaven from the earth, the waters above from the waters beneath, the earth from the seas. Having done that, He filled them with their respective contents: the heavens had the celestial bodies, the sun, the moon and the stars; the waters had the whales and sea-monsters, the sky the birds, and the earth the cattle and every creeping thing. Then, when every realm was occupied, God made man as the crown of His creation, to control, enjoy and care for it, and to share it all with Him.

This is important because it means that God did not start things off and then just wait to see what would happen. He is concerned for His world and especially for man as His carefully designed colleague.

2. *Man turned his back upon God*

Man's correct station in the universe is unique. He is intended to be higher than the animal creation, over which he has been given a responsibility, and yet he is to be subordinate to God. Genesis chapter 3 tells us how man could not bear this betwixt-and-between position. He wanted to be like God. He was deceived into thinking that he only had to disobey God's express command to become greater and wiser and more godlike. In trying to grow higher he in fact fell to a much lower estate. He had sinned against God and in a moment the whole of the created order was put out of true.

Such a perversion of God's good plan could not go unpunished. Man was driven out of his God-given domain in the garden of Eden and before many generations had passed the whole human race was, as it were, purged by the judgment of the Flood to give an opportunity for a fresh start to be made. Man's heart had not changed, however, and Noah's successors were not much better than the men and women who had preceded him.

□ Five Themes

The fresh start was eventually made, not with the whole of the human race, but with one family, the family of Abraham, and he was the central figure in the establishment of the old covenant. We can trace five distinctive themes which make up this teaching.

1. *God chose a people*

It has always been firmly rooted in Jewish thought that they are the chosen people of God. The idea stems from God's word to Abraham in Genesis 12: 3: "I will bless them that bless thee, and curse him that curseth thee: and in thee shall all families of the earth be blessed."

Other passages, too, show that Abraham was in a special relationship with God (Genesis 13: 14 ff.; 17: 19; 22: 16 ff.), and that his descendants shared that blessing with him. So, as children of Abraham, the whole Jewish race considered themselves the heirs of the promises made to their forefather; that they were God's chosen people; that other nations would be blessed through them; and that they were to be a light to the Gentiles round about.

This doctrine of election often led the Israelites into trouble, and they had to be warned by Ezekiel that it was not because of anything worthy in them that God had chosen them: He had done it "for His own name's sake".

In much the same way, the Christian believes that under the new covenant, he and his fellow-Christians have been called and chosen of God to belong to Him and to witness to His Name. "Ye have not chosen me, but I have chosen you", says Jesus to His disciples in every generation. The Christian doctrine of election is unpopular and often misunderstood—by the elect as well as by outsiders!—but it is basic to the agreement which God has made with His people.

2. God demanded obedience

Every agreement has its terms, and God's covenant with Abraham was no exception. On the one hand, He promised the blessing, and on the other hand He expected His laws to be obeyed. "The blessing" is almost a technical term, and it sums up everything that God gives to a person when His face is towards him; namely, prosperity and health of soul and body, honour in the eyes of other men and the supreme inward condition of 'peace', the state of harmony with God, the world and oneself.

The condition for the blessing was obedience and nothing could be substituted for it. This is well illustrated by an incident in the life of Saul described in 1 Samuel 15. As king of Israel, Saul had a prime duty to do as God commanded him without question. Through the prophet Samuel, Saul was told to fight against the Amalekites and utterly destroy them because they had incurred God's wrath and had to be punished. But that seemed wasteful to Saul and he thought he would keep back some of the spoil, making the excuse that he was going to use it to sacrifice to the Lord at Gilgal!

Samuel's rebuke indicates the unquestioning obedience which God demands of His followers: "Hath the Lord as great delight in burnt-offerings and sacrifices, as in obeying the voice of the Lord? Behold, to obey is better than sacrifice, and to hearken than the fat of rams. For rebellion is as the sin of witchcraft, and stubbornness is as iniquity and idolatry" (1 Samuel 15: 22 f.).

This obedience was to the Ten Commandments, which were the stipulations of the covenant as given to Moses, and to whatever else was God's revealed will. For Christians this means the teaching of the Bible and the guidance of the Holy Spirit, which we must obey just as unquestioningly if we are to know God's blessing on our lives.

This does not of course mean that if we obey God, everything in life becomes easy—perfect health, no worries, plenty of money and a knighthood for good measure! Old Testament believers soon learnt that God's favour was sometimes shown in suffering and pain, as Job found out. Often the wicked seemed to prosper at the expense of the godly, but ultimately it was seen that only the believer had the inner strength to face hardships and to triumph over them. The Psalmist wrote of men who "going through the vale of misery use it for a well". The blessing gave a man power to transform his circumstances. And what was true of the Old Testament is true also of the New.

3. *God's people failed miserably*

God's standards were high. He was not only the Creator God, He was the Holy One of Israel who judged His people righteously. Even though He was full of compassion and mercy, slow to anger and of great kindness, He could not lower His righteous standards to meet the requirements of sinful men. He did not expect fallen man to be perfect and sinless, but He did expect him to be humble: "For thus saith the high and lofty One that inhabiteth eternity, whose name is Holy: I dwell in the high and holy place, with him also that is of a contrite and humble spirit" (Isaiah 57: 15).

He wanted the humility of a man who admitted his sin and not the pride of the unrepentant: those who walked humbly with their God were acceptable to Him. They were not, however, the majority.

Mostly, they were "rebellious children", "a people laden with iniquity, a seed of evil-doers". They were either lifted up with self-confidence and self-righteousness, or they flagrantly disobeyed God's laws to suit their own purposes. It was the job of the prophets to depict unmistakably the wrongdoings of the people, and they often did this by accusing God's covenanted people of spiritual adultery and idolatry, flirting with other gods when they were bound in a spiritual union with Him.

Christians, too, commit spiritual adultery when they turn away from Christ to hanker after the world. James writes: "Ye adulterers, and adulteresses, know ye not that the friendship of the world is enmity with God?" (James 4: 4). And John adds a solemn postscript to his first Epistle: "Little children, keep yourselves from idols" (1 John 5: 21).

4. *God forgives*

The theme of forgiveness constantly recurs in the Old Testament. It first appears in Genesis 4: 6, when God says to Cain, who is angry with his brother, Abel, "Why art thou wroth? and why is thy countenance fallen? If thou doest well shalt thou not be accepted?" That is to say, "It is not too late to remedy your wrongdoing: if you do what is good and right, you can still be forgiven and return to favour."

The condition of forgiveness is repentance that shows itself by right conduct. The Hebrew was a practical man and no spiritual activity was ever completely abstract. For him "to repent" meant not just to feel sorry for his sins, but to live differently. This is the meaning which has been carried over into the New Testament and it is the meaning of repentance for the Christian today.

It is God's nature to forgive and to forget. God has a long memory and we often read of Him remembering His people, or of His people praying, "Remember me, O Lord". Again, to remember is no mere mental exercise: it has a practical side to it involving action and assistance. So when God says: "I, even I, am he that blotteth out thy transgressions for mine own sake, and will not remember thy sins" (Isaiah 43: 25), it means that He will not punish Israel's sins, for they are utterly erased from His memory.

5. God has a better way

An agreement which one party keeps and the other party is always breaking is not satisfactory. Some of the prophets saw this only too clearly and prophesied of a day when a new covenant would be made. So in Jeremiah 31: 31 ff: "Behold, the days come, saith the Lord, that I will make a new covenant with the house of Israel, and with the house of Judah: not according to the covenant that I made with their fathers, in the day that I took them by the hand to bring them out of the land of Egypt; which my covenant they brake, although I was an husband unto them, saith the Lord; but this shall be the covenant that I will make with the house of Israel . . . I will put my law in their inward parts, and write it in their hearts; and will be their God, and they shall be my people. And they shall teach no more every man his neighbour . . . saying, know the Lord: for they shall all know me . . . for I will forgive their iniquity, and I will remember their sin no more."

In great measure this has been fulfilled in the new covenant in Jesus Christ, whereby the Holy Spirit not only gives to Christians a new nature, so that they want to do God's will, but also enables them to do it. This is an immense step forward from the Old Covenant, and it is not surprising that the New Testament writings more than once compare the old with the new, regarding the old as the dead letter of the law and the new as a life-giving spirit (see Romans 7: 6; 2 Corinthians 3: 6).

There is, of course, much more to the new covenant than this, for it is centred in the coming of Jesus the Messiah and His death and resurrection for the sins of the whole world. Much of the Old Testament, consciously or even unconsciously, looks forward to Him and His coming, and so we conclude this chapter with a look at Christ in the Old Testament.

□ Christ in the Old Testament

The basic problem of all religion is the problem of human sin. How did it get into the world? Can a good God allow it? Must it be punished or can it be forgiven?

The Old Testament starts with this problem and deals with it on every page. At the very beginning it

83

tells how sin entered the world, and in the same sentence it tells how one day sin would be defeated. "And the Lord God said unto the serpent . . . I will put enmity between thee and the woman, and between thy seed and her seed; it shall bruise thy head, and thou shalt bruise his heel" (Genesis 3: 14 f.).

This was a verse which brought considerable encouragement to the Old Testament reader, because he knew that the powers of evil would not be finally triumphant but that God would raise up a Saviour who would defeat Satan once and for all even though He himself was bruised in the process. How it would happen he did not fully know, but he was given a number of indications. Here are three.

1. The Lamb of God

As far back as Genesis chapter 22, this clue could be seen. Abraham was offering up his promised son, Isaac, on a hilltop in Mount Moriah (where later the city of Jerusalem, the Temple and the Cross of Calvary were to be). At the last moment, the angel of the Lord stayed Abraham's hand and showed him that God had provided a sacrifice, a ram caught by its horns in a thicket. In place of Isaac a substitute had been found.

Years later, when Moses was being prepared to lead the children of Israel out of Egypt into the promised land, God plagued the Egyptians with many judgments and the last of these was the Passover, and the death of all the first-born. On this occasion, Moses and the children of Israel were told how to protect themselves against the destroying angel. Each family was to take a lamb out of the flock, kill it, roast the meat and eat it indoors, while the blood was to be smeared upon the lintel and doorposts of their house outside. The angel would see the blood of the sacrificed lamb and "pass over". Once again, a substitute had been found to save the people.

This same idea of a sacrificial animal was at the root of all the offerings described in the early chapters of Leviticus. The man who came to God offered a sacrifice to atone for his sins and laid his hand on the head of the innocent victim as it was killed, as if to identify himself with it, so that it might be thought that the sacrificed animal was bearing the sinner's guilt. In this way the Israelite began to appreciate both the severity of God's judgment upon sin, and also the grace of God in allowing for the death of a substitute instead, two lessons that were demonstrated supremely as Jesus Christ, the Lamb of God, bore our sins in His body on the Cross.

2. *The King of David's Line*

At first quite unrelated to this idea was the promise given to David that his house and his kingdom would be established for ever: a promise which was repeated to Solomon his son and never forgotten by subsequent generations. The prophets were particularly conscious of it: Isaiah wrote: "There shall come forth a rod out of the stem of Jesse, and a branch shall grow out of his roots: and the spirit of the Lord shall rest upon him . . ." (11: 1 f.). The "branch" of the family of

85

David was to be the chosen king of the Jewish people. He would rule in righteousness and truth. In his days Israel would be glorious, and the Gentiles would seek after him. His reign would be a reign of peace, for he would be a man of peace.

Already we have the picture of the coming Messiah–Christ, for the words 'Christ' and 'Messiah' are identical, being the Greek and Hebrew words meaning 'the Anointed One'. This anointed, chosen king was to be everything that the people could wish for. "His name shall be called Wonderful Counsellor, Mighty God, Everlasting Father, Prince of Peace" (Isaiah 9: 6). The thought of a peaceful ruler was not only Isaiah's. Zechariah too prophesied His coming: "Rejoice greatly, O daughter of Zion: shout, O daughter of Jerusalem: behold, thy king cometh unto thee: he is just, and having salvation; lowly, and riding upon an ass, and upon a colt, the foal of an ass" (Zechariah 9: 9).

3. *The Suffering Servant*

The theme that was to join together these two unrelated ideas of the Lamb of God bearing away sins and the Davidic Messiah ruling in peace and righteousness was the Suffering Servant found in Isaiah 42 to 53. Here we are introduced to the character of a servant of the Lord whose lot it will be to represent his people and innocently to suffer for them, bearing their iniquities and dying for their sins. "He was wounded for our transgressions, he was bruised for our iniquities: upon him was the chastisement that made us whole, and with his stripes we are healed ... Therefore I will divide him a portion with the great, and he shall divide the spoil with the strong; because he poured out his soul to death, and was numbered with the transgressors: yet he bore the sin of many, and made intercession for the transgressors" (Isaiah 53: 5, 12).

These words are a remarkable anticipation of the sufferings of Christ, and there is reason to believe that our Lord recognised their application to His death, and meditated upon them in the last days of His life on earth (cf. Luke 22: 37).

Other passages too seem to refer to a suffering Messiah. In Zechariah, for instance, we find reference to the wounds of Christ: "And if one asks him, What are these wounds in thine hands? Then he shall answer, Those with which I was wounded in the house of my friends" (13: 6). "And they shall look upon him whom they have pierced, and they shall mourn for him, as one mourneth for his only son (12: 10).

Once it was established in the Christian Church that the crucified Jesus and the promised Messiah were identical, many other Old Testament references were seen to apply prophetically to Christ. On the basis of Micah 5: 2, Bethlehem had always been regarded as the Messiah's birthplace (after all, it was David's own city), but the strange prophecy of a virgin birth in Isaiah 7: 14 was also seen to apply to the miraculous circumstances that surrounded Mary's conception.

The crucifixion, too, brought new meaning into Psalm 22 as the Crucifixion psalm, and countless other passages were re-read in the light of Jesus' ministry, death and resurrection. The similarities are too great to be coincidences, and we can only conclude that God has given in the Old Testament not only specific prophecies of the Anointed One that He was going to send, but also a number of verbal clues which could be interpreted with special reference to some aspect of His life.

The Old Testament is thus a preparation for the New Testament in two senses. First, it tells of man's failure to keep God's laws and of the breakdown of the old covenant, which leads on to God's determination to institute a new and better covenant on a different basis. Secondly, it looks forward to the coming of the Christ who would be the mediator of this new covenant and whose kingdom would be the ideal place where every thing that was good would flourish, and where sin would be done away with for ever. It is against this background that the Old Testament needs to be read.

6 TWO SUGGESTIONS

The whole purpose of this little
Guide is to help people to read their Old Testaments.
We have seen why and how it should be read. We
have breathed something of its atmosphere. We have
looked at its history, its contents and its general
message. But all this is no substitute for actually
reading it as it is. To read or not to read, that is now
the question.

In hope that the answer is 'to read', we are adding
two suggested courses of reading so that you can get
to know this most fascinating part of God's revelation to His people.

As we said in chapter 1, the Old Testament needs
to be read in fair-sized portions and not just in chapters. The ideal is to take a book at a time, but some
of the longer ones may take nearly two hours to read,
and we do not all have the time or the concentration
to do that.

The following schemes are both divided into
twenty-six weeks. In scheme 'A' each week is given
enough reading for one or two hours. You can either

divide it up on the basis of ten to fifteen minutes a day, or you can have two or three longer sessions in the course of the week instead. If you like, you can do two weeks' reading in one and so halve the length of the course. This is up to you.

The aim is to cover the ground. You are not at this stage trying to study the Old Testament, nor are you reading it to get help devotionally. You are simply getting acquainted with what it contains. So you will not hesitate to skip passages where you find repetitions or catalogues of names, and in some cases chapters which can conveniently be omitted have been noted.

We have generally kept to the framework of the historical order, but have inserted some poetry or prophecy now and again for the sake of variety. Do use the Revised Standard Version if you can—its clear translation will save you hours, and will make the reading much more enjoyable for you.

No mention has been made of the Psalms. This is because of the suggestion already given that they should be read one a day over a period of five months, and they could possibly be combined with this six-month course of reading.

Finally, if you are a slow reader and a real beginner in the Old Testament, don't get discouraged at the apparent vastness of scheme 'A'. The alternative scheme 'B' has been specially designed with the newcomer in mind. Try that for a start. You will not cover the whole of the Old Testament but you will dip into nearly every book and perhaps when you have got to the end of it you will start again on scheme 'A' and tackle the real thing. A selection of psalms has been added but you may prefer to be reading a psalm a day.

Our aim in both courses is not to start the reader on a marathon that he will never be able to keep up, but to give a planned system of reading in which the goal is visible and well worth attaining.

"He who gives heed to the word will prosper, and happy is he who trusts in the Lord."

Scheme 'A'

Week		No. of chapters
1	Genesis 1–25	25
2	Genesis 26–50	25
3	Exodus (omit 21–23, 25–31)	30
4	Leviticus 1–10; Numbers (omit 1–5, 7, 26–30)	35
5	Deuteronomy	34
6	Isaiah 1–14, 24–30	21
7	Isaiah 40–66	27
8	Joshua	24
9	Judges; Ruth	25
10	Job (omit 8–18; 20–37); Ecclesiastes	25
11	1 Samuel	31
12	2 Samuel	24
13	Amos; Hosea; Micah	30
14	1 Kings	22
15	2 Kings	25
16	Jeremiah 1–25	25
17	Jeremiah 26–45, 52; Lamentations	26
18	Jonah; Nahum; Zephaniah; Habakkuk	13
19	1 Chronicles 10–29	20
20	2 Chronicles 1–16	16
21	2 Chronicles 17–36	20
22	Ezekiel (omit 25–32, 40–48)	31
23	Daniel; Esther	22
24	Ezra; Nehemiah	23
25	Obadiah; Joel; Haggai; Zechariah; Malachi	24
26	Proverbs (omit 10–29); Song of Solomon	19

Scheme 'B'
(Beginners)

Week		Psalm	No. of chapters
1	Genesis 1–3, 15–19, 22	1	10
2	Genesis 24–27, 37, 39–41	8	9
3	Exodus 1–4, 11–17	15	12
4	Exodus 20, 24, 32; Numbers 11–14	16	8
5	Deuteronomy 1–8	19	9
6	Isaiah 6–12	22	8
7	Isaiah 40–44, 49–53	23	11
8	Joshua 1–8	24	9
9	Judges 1–2, 6–7, 13–16; Ruth	27	13
10	Job 1–3, 38–39, 42; Ecclesiastes 3, 11–12	34	10
11	1 Samuel 1–3, 10–11, 16–20	42, 43	12
12	2 Samuel 6–7, 11–12, 18, 23–24	51	8
13	Amos 1–5; Hosea 1–3	73	9
14	1 Kings 3, 8–10, 17–19	84	8
15	2 Kings 1–5, 22–23	90	8
16	Jeremiah 1, 20, 27–29; Lamentations 1	92	7
17	Jeremiah 36–43	96	9
18	Jonah; Habakkuk	103	8
19	1 Chronicles 22, 28–29; 2 Chronicles 29–32	111	8
20	Ezekiel 1–5, 33–34, 37	116	9
21	Daniel 1–7	121	8
22	Ezra 7–10; Nehemiah 1–5, 8	122	11